DAD,
I wrote a
book about
you

Dear Dad,

I wrote a book about you. But I didn't do it alone. Because the history and the antics and the experiences I wanted to capture are ones we created together. So it was easy to go back through all of those wonderful memories and come up with enough for a book.

I think it turned out pretty well. It helps, of course, that I was writing about one of my favorite subjects. Because in my book, Dad, you're the greatest.

Love,

I know it SOUNDS SILLY now, but FOR A LONG TiME,

HEY, DAD!

You make it LOOK SO eASy, BUt, just the Same,

You're the most

PERSON I KNOW.

You may NEVER get me to SAY this out LOUD, but...

it turns out
you were *actually*
RIGHT ABOUT

There's a favorite photograph in my mind. It's a PICTURE of you.

You're here:

and you're wearing:

and the year is probably:

and just thinking about it
makes me feel:

Of all the
millions
of faTHers
in the world,

You might Be the
ONLY ONE who

I inherited
your

World's
most

DAD

If there's a food that *always* makes me THINK OF YOU, it's

And if there's a SONG that BRINGS BACK a GOOD MEMORY, it's

And if there's a PLACE in the WORLD that will ALWAYS BE YOURS, it's

It's pretty much GUARANTEED that future generations in our family will know all about...

YOUR LEGENDARY

I don't know if I ever told you this, but I used to think it was the GREATEST TREAT IN THE WORLD WHEN YOU'D

You've probably forgotten ALL ABOUT THiS, But...

oNe of my
fAVORite
MeMorieS
is that Time we

If I hAD to get Scientific about it,

I'd say
You're
made
up of
EQUAL
ParTs:

I KNOW I didn't appreciate it at the time, But, LOOKING BACK, I'm amazed by HOW MUCH EFFORT you used to put into

_____

and you

did it for me.

THANK YOU.

Before

YOU HAD ME,
YOU USED TO

Let's face it, you've always BEEN COOL.

I'm totally certain that THE WHOLE WORLD WOULD Be a better place...

when I WAS LittLe, I THOUGHT you Were

Now that I'M OLDER, I THINK you are

UM, I think YOU PROBABLY DESERVE THIS. →

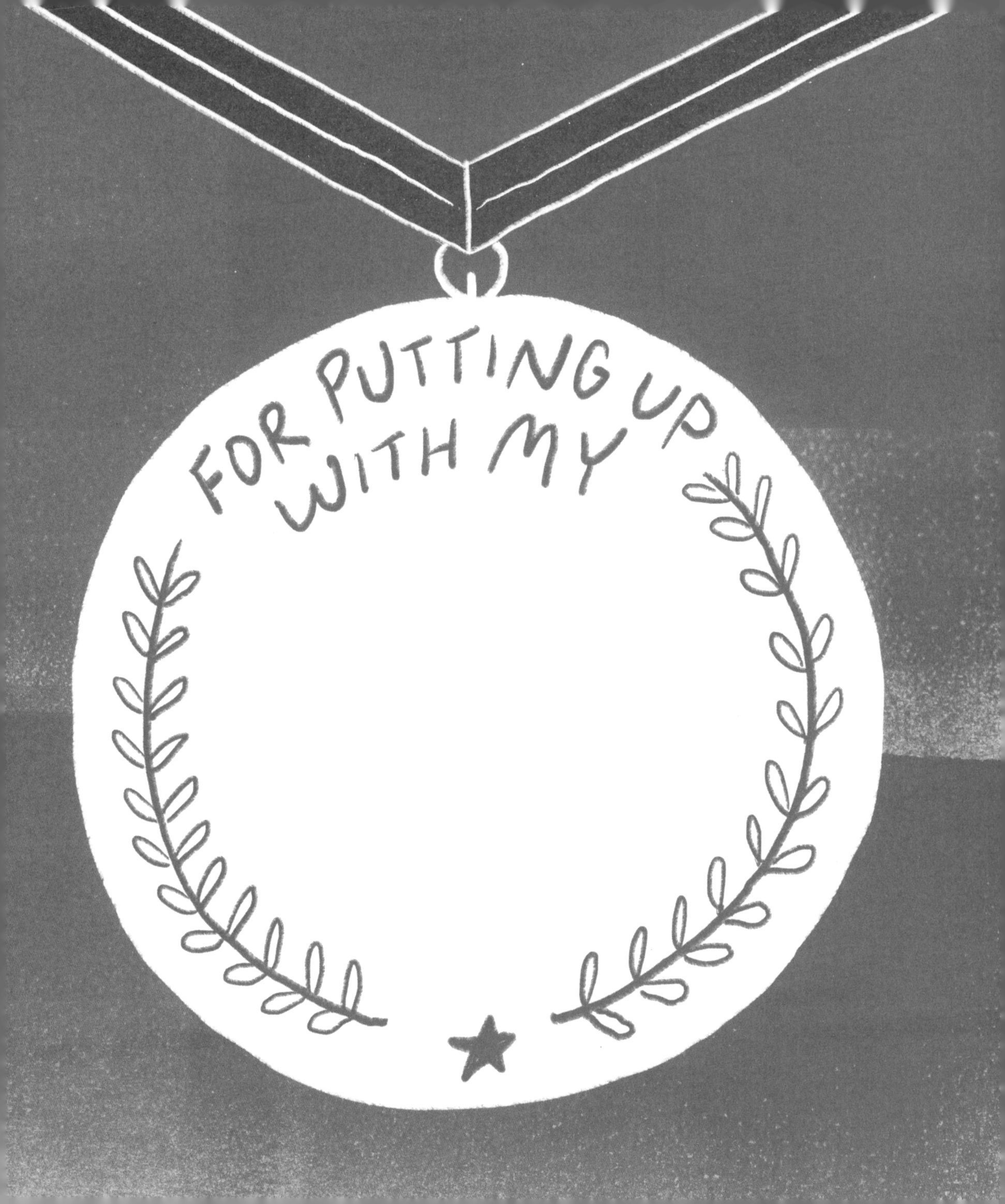
FOR PUTTING UP
WITH MY

EVERYONE
I know
THINKS it's so
incredible
THAT YOU

AND I have
to admit it:

THEY'RE RIGHT.

I love that the OLDER I GET, the OUR RELATIONSHIP becomes.

Just consider this
your personal
HALL of FaMe,
WHICH CONTAINS:

Your most
REMaRKaBLE
AchieveMENT

Your
wisest
piece OF
ADVICE

Your Most
FAMOUS
Saying

I hope we *never* lose the

____

WE SHARE.

Whenever I think about the time we

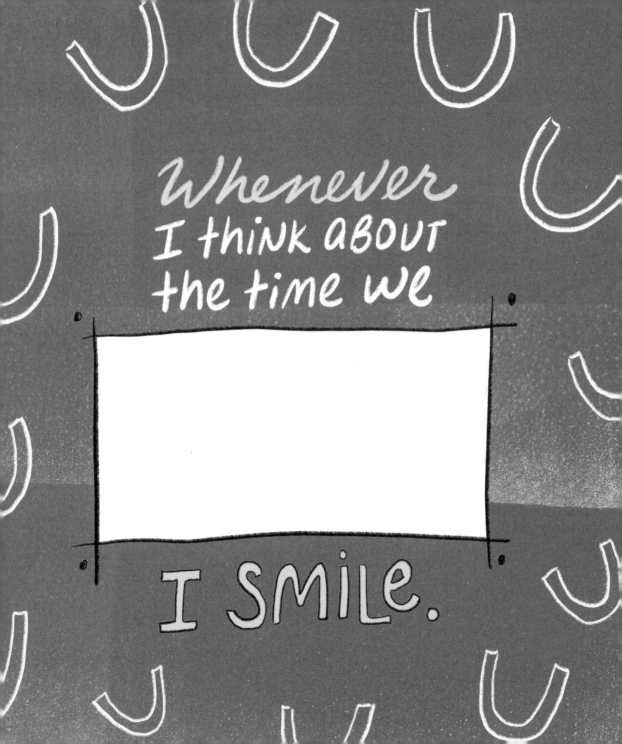

I smile.

I Realized a LITTLE WHILE AGO that you're EVEN MORE

than I knew.

WHEN THEY finally MAKE A MOVIE OF YOUR LIFE...

HeRe's WHAT it WiLL Be CALLeD:

AND HeRe's WHO WiLL PLAY the STARRiNG ROLe:

THe SOUND TRACK WiLL feature:

AND the CRiTiCS WiLL SAY:

I'm COMPLETELY certain that...

HAVING YOU as
MY DAD
Has made me

If I could
Leave You with just
one thing
to REMEMBER,
always and
FOREVER,
it would Be that...

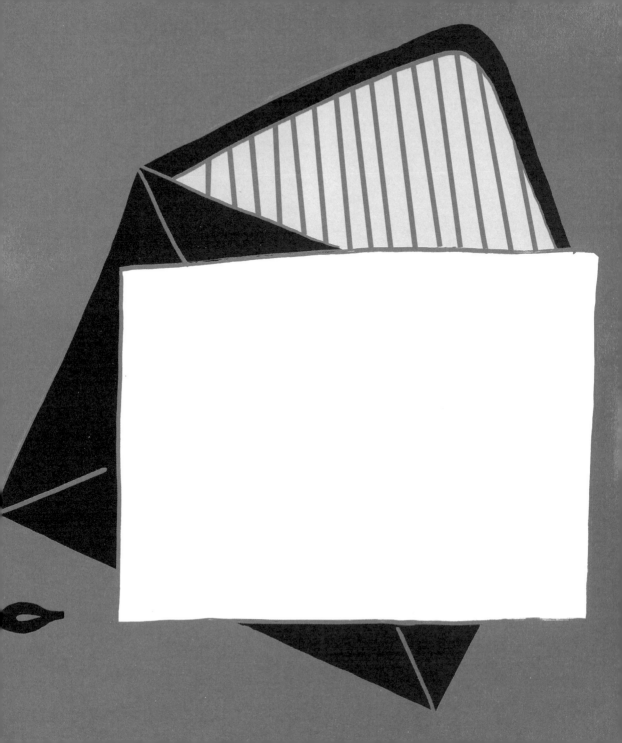

COMPENDIUM®
live inspired

Actually
Written By:

Written By: M.H. Clark

Designed & Illustrated By: Justine Edge

Edited By: Ruth Austin

With SPECIAL THANKS to the ENTIRE COMPENDIUM family.

ISBN: 978-1-946873-34-7
Library of Congress Control Number: 2018941327

1st printing. Printed in China with soy and metallic inks.